For my family, particularly my mom.

Simply Elegant Napkin Folding

CHRIS JORDAN

Sterling Publishing Co., Inc. New York
A Sterling/Tamos Book

A Sterling / Tamos Book
© 2000 Chris Jordan

Sterling Publishing Co., Inc.
387 Park Avenue South, New York, NY 10016

Tamos Books Inc.
300 Wales Avenue, Winnipeg, MB, Canada R2M 2S9

10   9   8   7   6   5   4   3   2   1

Distributed in Canada by Sterling Publishing Co., Inc.
c/o Canadian Manda Group, 1 Atlantic Avenue, Suite 105
Toronto, Ontario, Canada M6K 3E7
Distributed in Great Britain and Europe by Cassell PLC
Wellington House, 125 Strand, London WC2R 0BB, England
Distributed in Australia by Capricorn Link (Australia) Pty Ltd.
P.O. Box 6651, Baulkham Hills,
Business Centre, NSW 2153, Australia

Design   Norman Schmidt
Photography   Jerry Grajewski
Special thanks to Moulé in Winnipeg, Canada, for their contributions to
table settings.

Printed in China

CANADIAN CATALOGING IN PUBLICATION DATA

Jordan, Chris, 1954-

Simply elegant napkin folding

"A Sterling/Tamos book."
Includes index.
ISBN 1-895569-52-4

1. Napkin folding.   I. Title.

TX879.J67 1999   642'.7   C99-920050-X

LIBRARY OF CONGRESS CATALOGING IN PUBLICATION DATA

Jordan, Chris.

Data available.

Tamos Books Inc. acknowledges the financial support of the Government of Canada through the Book
Publishing Industry Development Program (BPIDP) for our publishing activities.

ISBN 1-895569-52-4

TABLE OF CONTENTS

INTRODUCTION

DINING has always been a fun experience, but it wasn't always elegant. In medieval times each diner came to the table with his own pointed knife (for cutting off and stabbing chunks of food), spoon, and drinking cup. There were no plates. Instead, trenches of bread were used to sop up the juices of mutton, game, and fish. Greasy fingers were usually wiped on clothing. When tables of the rich began to be covered with fine linens and silks laid with corner points hanging, these convenient appendages were often tucked under the chin of the diner to catch food bits and used to clean the face and hands, probably to the horror of the hostess, who had no easy laundry facilities.

About the 15th Century in Europe large pieces of cloth began to be used at table to wipe face and hands during the meal, and these table napkins could be washed and reused. As knives and forks replaced fingers the need for napkins declined, but when the edges of tablecloths were once again employed to wipe sticky fingers, napkins assumed a more permanent role. Gradually cloth napkins took on additional duties. They wrapped a bottle of wine while pouring in order to catch any drips that would otherwise mar the tablecloth. They protected the hostess' hands from being burned while passing hot serving platters. They kept food warm (breads or dinner rolls, baked potatoes, or even pie) as it was waiting to be eaten.

In the days before modern conveniences, napkins used for family dining were reused for several meals before being laundered. After each use, the cloth napkin was carefully folded and set aside for the next use. To assure that each family member continued to use the same napkin, each person folded their napkin a different way to distinguish it as their own. Eventually the folds became more and more elaborate and were given names. The names varied depending on the geographic area, but the designs spread and were shared among women who were quick to see the beauty that these simple pieces of cloth added to often drab eating surroundings. The napkin, along with other table linens, became a means for women to display their artistic expertise. They adorned napkins with intricate laces and embroidery, created artful stitching, and learned to fold them in unique designs. As society became more affluent, fine china and gleaming silver were used in table settings, which were enriched by elegantly folded napkins in engraved napkin rings. Napkins were always functional. Later they added elegance to table decor and displayed the artistry of the hostess.

Today is no exception. Even at a time of pre-packaged, plain paper disposables, the napkin is still not purely functional. It can be a decorating tool, essential to define the mood of the festive table setting. Paper napkins now come in beautiful colors and prints and a good fold gives them additional appeal. However, cloth napkins have never lost their special elegance and can even be family heirlooms. Both can be folded artfully for any occasion with remarkable decorating effect. A beautifully set table adds warmth and richness to any dining area. Carefully folded napkins help create a distinctive touch. You can accomplish any of the fabulous designs shown in this book very easily. Simply master the basic steps on the beginning pages, then follow the step-by-step directions for the design you choose.

This book is organized progressively by technique. If you start at the beginning and progress through each fold and technique, you will see how the most intricate looking designs are actually nothing more than combinations of the elementary basic manipulations of folds. You'll be amazed how easy it is to master even the most complicated looking arrangements. With this book at your side you can make simply elegant folded napkins for memorable table settings to delight your family and guests.

BASIC FOLDING TIPS

1. Always lay napkin on clean, flat surface to fold. Pressed and starched napkins make sharper creases. Do not iron the folds in place – finger press them firmly for a soft and luxurious look.

2. Most napkin folding designs require a square napkin. More complex designs are more successful with a larger napkin. Intricately folded small napkins require more skill but are show-stoppers every time.

3. Practice with a cloth napkin that is fairly stiff. Use your ironing board as a table and keep iron handy to "erase" folds and start over if needed. Use a napkin with an obvious right and wrong side. This makes it easier to follow instructions until the folds are mastered.

4. Choose cloth or paper napkins for the finished napkin design. Because it holds a crease so well, a paper napkin is easy to fold and consistently holds its shape. The finished designs are crisp and neat. Choose three-ply paper napkins in solid colors with a design on the entire napkin. Since paper is so fragile and spots so easily, be sure your hands are clean and absolutely dry before handling. Many paper napkins are not perfectly square, so be sure to check the dimensions on the package. You may be able to trim them neatly. Most folding designs in this book adapt very well to the paper napkin. Cloth napkins are luxurious, elegant, and reusable. Designs made with cloth napkins have a softer look and are the perfect choice to use with napkin rings or to display in a glass where they can flow and spread. Cloth napkins need to be laundered and stored (p 94). Cloth napkins do not have pre-folds as do paper napkins and therefore are easier to design. They also sit comfortably on the lap, do not slide to the floor so easily, and are stronger than paper, to prevent food seepage on clothing.

BASIC FOLDING TECHNIQUES

ALL fold designs begin with a flat napkin folded into a square, rectangle, or triangle. All the folds in this book are derived from these basic folds. If you do not have space that allows you to store your cloth napkins flat, you can give yourself a head start by storing them already folded into these beginning shapes.

From these basic folds you simply add a few elementary folding techniques to produce almost any design. You can continue to fold it, roll it, knot it, or accordion pleat it. These are simple skills. It is nothing more than combinations of these that result in the most difficult napkin folds. Once you have mastered these skills you can use the techniques to develop fold designs of your own creation. Even your children can help.

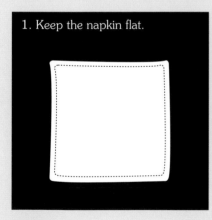

1. Keep the napkin flat.

SQUARE
A square starting shape is achieved in one of three ways.

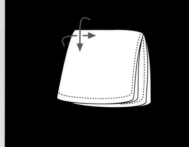

2. Basic quarterfold square – fold from left to right and then top to bottom.

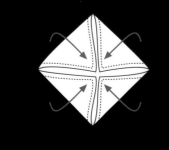

3. Centerpoint square – fold each corner point into the center.

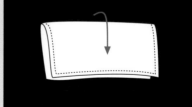

1. One-half rectangle – fold the napkin in half from left to right or top to bottom (directions may be reversed depending on where the open edges need to be).

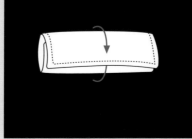

2. One-third rectangle – fold the napkin into thirds.

RECTANGLE
A rectangle starting shape has two basic steps.

TRIANGLE
A triangle can be formed in two ways.

PLEATED

1. One-half triangle – match a corner point to the opposite corner.

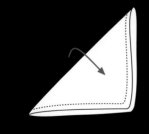

1. Accordian pleated – Lay the napkin flat. Fold the bottom edge up about an inch or an inch and a half. Finger press. Flip the napkin over and fold this top folded edge down the same width. Finger press. Continue in this manner until the napkin is a strip of accordion pleats. (You can also complete this process without repeatedly turning the napkin over. Keep holding the edges with your index finger while turning under the pleats.)

2. Quarterfold triangle – fold it again for a smaller triangle. This is the basic quarter triangle fold.

Try to measure the folds so that the last fold goes the same direction as the first. This way the open edges are facing the same direction.

Basic folds from squares

ALL the folds pictured here begin with one of the basic square folds. By following the examples and trying the suggestions for some variations, you may create other designs that start from squares.

FLIP FOLD

These different flip folds are simple progressions from the quarterfold square.

1. Start with a quarterfold square (p9) and turn it diagonally. Flip one corner back toward the corner fold point.

2. Flip two corners back toward the corner fold point.

3. Flip three corners back toward the corner fold point.

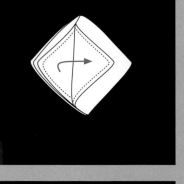

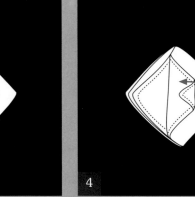

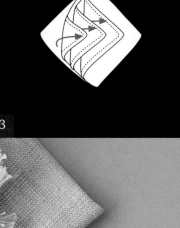

4. VARIATION. Fold the flipped corners to meet the middle fold line. This forms a second set of smaller triangle flips (see below).

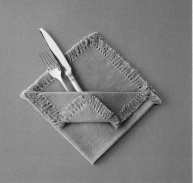

DOUBLE DIAMOND

This fold begins in the same way as the Flip Fold. After forming the double diamond shapes, you can add two extra folds to produce a striking hexagon shape. The vertical nature of this design allows it to be set atop or beside the plate.

1. Start with a quarterfold square (p9) and turn it diagonally with open corners at the top. Fold upper layer down to meet the bottom folded corner point and back again to meet the center line.

2. Take the top corner of the next layer and fold it down to meet the center line.

3. To make the hexagon, fold the left corner underneath the napkin to the center point of the back of the napkin. Fold the right corner underneath in a like manner to form a hexagon.

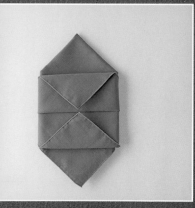

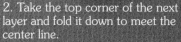

1

2

3

TRIANGLE FLIP

This is a fun fold to use for striped or geometric print napkins.

1. Start with a quarterfold square (p9) and turn it diagonally so that open corners are at the bottom and the folded edge is at the top right. Then fold the right corner to the left corner.

2. Fold left corner of the top layer to the right. It can be taken either to meet the long edge of the triangle or over the edge, as shown.

3. Fold the next layer from left to right so that some of the first layer still shows. Finally fold the last layer from left to right again, still exposing some of the underneath layer.

NOTE You may need to press the last fold in place if you are working with a heavy napkin.

WALLET OR HOT MAT

This fold is virtually indestructible – it won't come unfolded without help. Use it as a hot mat for serving dishes or a cover for stained spots on your tablecloth. If you put serving spoons, salt and pepper shakers, or even flowers on it, no one will ever know. Turn the hot mat over and it becomes a wallet complete with a top pocket.

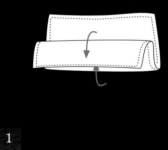

1. Place the napkin flat on the table with the right or print side of the napkin facing you and bring the bottom edge to the top. Then fold the top layer down to the bottom folded edge.

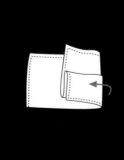

2. Flip the napkin over, keeping the open edge at the top. Then fold the napkin in thirds by bringing the right edge two-thirds of the way to the left.

flip over before folding

3. Fold the left edge over to the right folded edge.

4. Bring the top edges down to the bottom. There is now a pocket at the top edge. Pick up the napkin with your thumbs on the front side and your fingers inside the pocket. Turn the pocket INSIDE OUT. Sharpen the corners by poking them from the inside.

Flip it over and slip a flower, picture, or money into the pocket of the wallet.

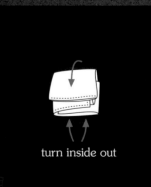

turn inside out

SEASHELL

The depth produced from these beautifully layered folds makes this a particularly good choice for a polyester blend napkin. Plain, single color napkins will highlight the intricate folds that look complicated but are not.

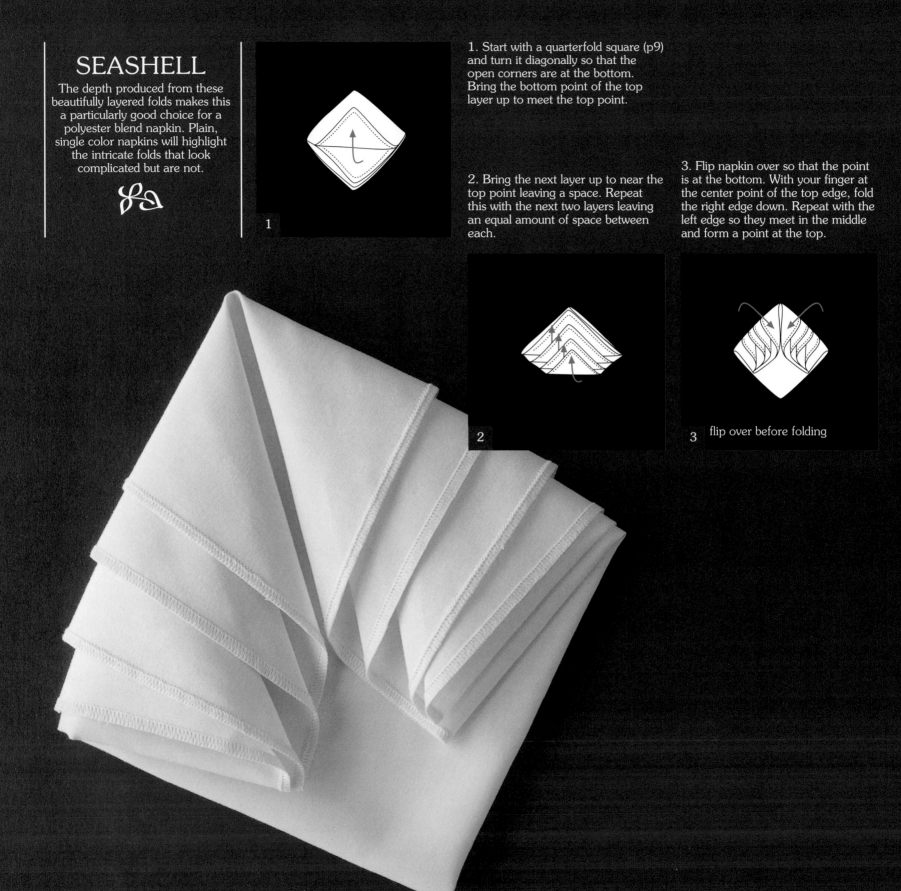

1. Start with a quarterfold square (p9) and turn it diagonally so that the open corners are at the bottom. Bring the bottom point of the top layer up to meet the top point.

2. Bring the next layer up to near the top point leaving a space. Repeat this with the next two layers leaving an equal amount of space between each.

3. Flip napkin over so that the point is at the bottom. With your finger at the center point of the top edge, fold the right edge down. Repeat with the left edge so they meet in the middle and form a point at the top.

1

2

3   flip over before folding

ARROWHEAD

This variation of Seashell is perfect
for two napkins of contrasting
colors. It can rest on the plate, at
its side, or stand proudly in a
napkin ring.

Follow steps 1 and 2 for Seashell,
(p16). Then fold the left corner to the
back forming a horizontal line across
the bottom. Fold the right side to the
back keeping the bottom horizontal
line even.

VARIATION
This design looks great with the small
corner at the top.

1

WRAP

This is another variation of Seashell. It can lie flat or stand on its own.

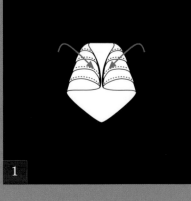

1. Follow steps 1 and 2 for Seashell, (p16). Flip napkin over so that the point is at the bottom. Then fold the sides, as shown.

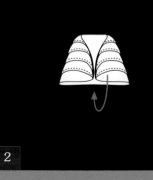

2. Fold the bottom triangle under the napkin. This will form a stand to hold the napkin up. Open the sides slightly for support if needed.

QUILT TRIANGLE

The split down the middle of this napkin design reminds me of the square of a quilt block that has been stitched down the middle. This fold is a great choice for buffet-style entertaining. A variety of patterned and colored napkins can be used. They can be folded and stacked to resemble ever changing quilt blocks. When one is removed it only serves to change the pattern of the remaining display.

3. Grasp the sides with your thumb and forefinger on top and make a beginning fold in between them. Then hold the center points to fold under. Straighten any crooked folds and fold the right edge to meet the left.

1. Lay the napkin on the table with the wrong side facing you and fold it into a centerpoint square (p9). Napkin must be perfectly square. Rotate the napkin so that it is still horizontal.

2. Fold the top half of the square down and underneath to make a rectangle.

LOTUS BLOSSOM

The Lotus Blossom is essentially a series of folds making centerpoint squares (p9). The three-dimensional qualities of this exquisite flower make it a conversation piece. You can add a fresh flower to the center for impact or place a mint or name card there. Simple folding and some careful manipulation of the petals is all that it takes to produce this striking blossom.

3. Flip the napkin over carefully, keeping the center points in place.

NOTE Slide one hand under and hold the top center points with the other (as a sandwich) and flip it over.

Again fold the corners of this new square into the center.

flip over before folding

3

pull from underneath

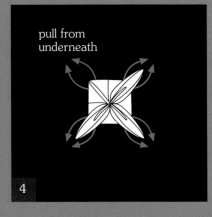

4

1. Lay the napkin on the table with the wrong side facing you and fold it into a centerpoint square (p9).

2. Fold the corners of this new square into the center to form a second, smaller centerpoint square. Hold the points firmly when bringing them into the center.

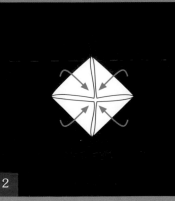

1

2

4. Hold the center point down firmly with one hand, reach underneath and gently pull a corner of the underneath layer out until it sits up and frames the corner of the top layer. Repeat for each corner.

NOTE The Lotus Blossom is easier in paper but looks most spectacular in cloth. A large napkin is best, but a 15 in or 16 in is easier to maneuver.

CHAPTER TWO

Basic folds from rectangles

Remember that the rectangle is just another form of the square.
You can experiment with the square designs by starting them from rectangles
to create different designs.

*A*LL the folds pictured here begin by folding the napkin
into a rectangle. You can see from the wide variety
in the completed designs that you cannot always
discern what shape a napkin design begins with by
looking at the outcome.

FOUR FLIPS

Just a quick flip of a neatly folded rectangle can add a large measure of elegance.

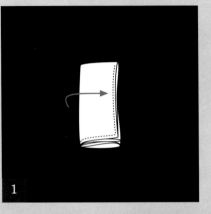

1. Start with a basic quarterfold square (p9). Fold it in half again to form a rectangle. Be sure the open corners are at the lower right corner.

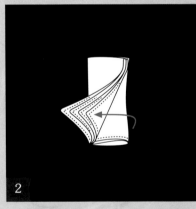

2. Take the open corners and flip them over to the left. They can be staggered for more effect.

SCARF

This design is perfect for napkins with a border design or fringed edges, since all of the free edges are exposed. The scarf can lay flat as a geometric design. Turned sideways, it resembles a jet fighter plane and would be great for a boy's birthday party. It also looks great in a napkin ring.

Different versions of this fold are achieved mainly by the final placement. Try setting it horizontally, or even upside down.

1. Place the napkin flat on the table with the wrong side facing up and bring the bottom edge over the top edge by about one inch.

NOTE By not folding the napkin exactly in half, the bottom and top layer are both emphasized and depth is added.

2. Holding your finger at the midpoint of the bottom edge, fold the lower right corner to the center line. Repeat with the lower left corner.

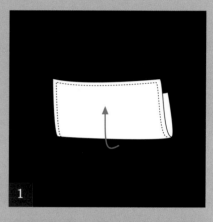

3. Fold the right edge to this center line and repeat with the left. Sharpen the bottom point if needed, or slide the bottom point through a napkin ring.

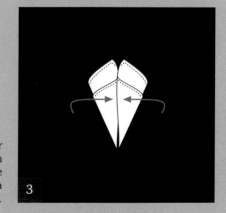

FLIGHT

The turned down wings on this fold suggest its name. Wherever you place it on the place setting (or cover), it will always be ready to take off. Using a crisp napkin and a napkin ring will help insure the best results.

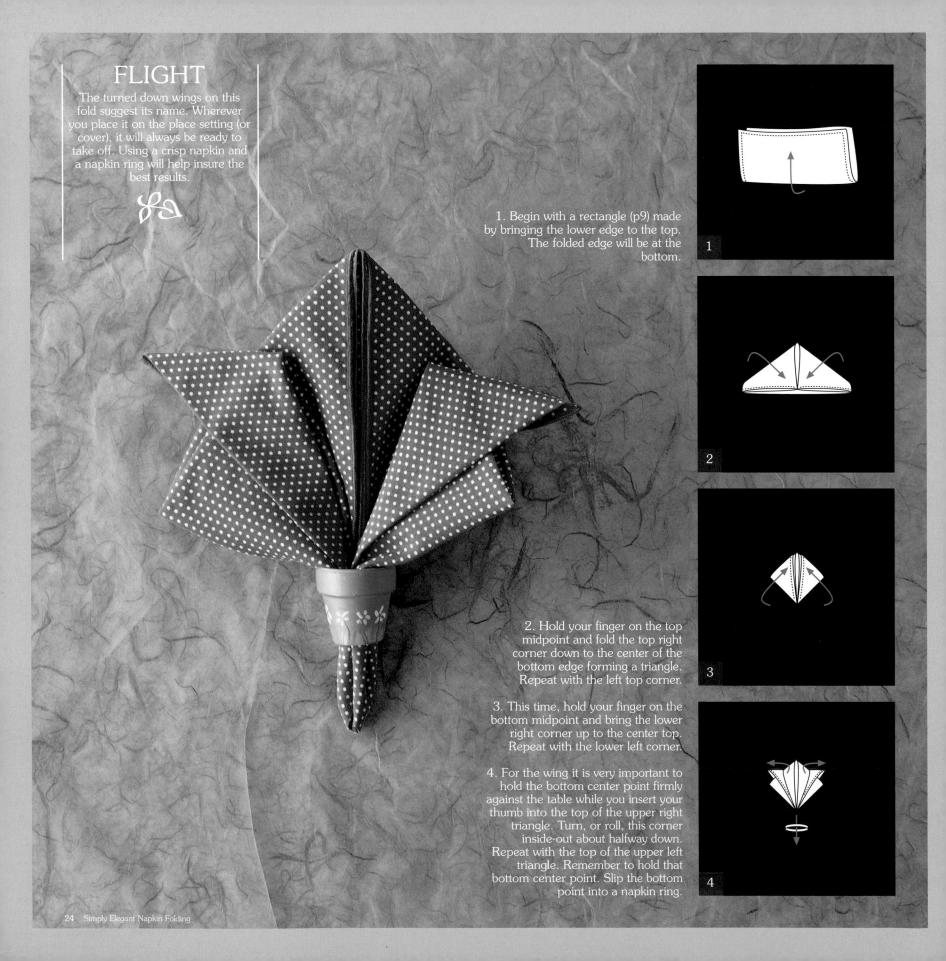

1. Begin with a rectangle (p9) made by bringing the lower edge to the top. The folded edge will be at the bottom.

2. Hold your finger on the top midpoint and fold the top right corner down to the center of the bottom edge forming a triangle. Repeat with the left top corner.

3. This time, hold your finger on the bottom midpoint and bring the lower right corner up to the center top. Repeat with the lower left corner.

4. For the wing it is very important to hold the bottom center point firmly against the table while you insert your thumb into the top of the upper right triangle. Turn, or roll, this corner inside-out about halfway down. Repeat with the top of the upper left triangle. Remember to hold that bottom center point. Slip the bottom point into a napkin ring.

TRIANGLE TUCK

If you were going to master only one fold, I would suggest this one, since it is one of the most versatile. These wonderful triangles can be used in buffet displays or even as hot mats. Tuck a card or flower into the side and it looks attractive anywhere on the cover setting.

1. Begin with a rectangle (p9) made by bringing the lower edge to the top. Hold your finger on the bottom midpoint and fold the bottom right corner UP to the center of the top edge.

2. Now fold the top left corner DOWN to the center of the bottom edge.

3. Hold your finger on the bottom midpoint and fold the left corner UP along the center line.

5. This new triangle has an opening at the top right edge. Take the upper right corner point from the remaining napkin part and tuck it inside the top edge of this triangle as far as you can. Straighten any corners.

4. Take this left triangle and fold it straight OVER the center line, forming a triangle.

CORNUCOPIA

The Triangle Tuck goes three-dimensional and turns into a Cornucopia that can be filled to overflowing for any feast.

1

Use the finished Triangle Tuck (p25). Holding it by the top point, stand it up along the long edge (large opening at left). Push the center point down just enough so that the cornucopia will sit by itself. Fill the opening with flowers, candy, novelties, or anything you would like.

TRI-FOLD

For a more formal occasion use this Tri-Fold design. The fold is small enough not to distract from beautiful china and silver place settings. It can even add to the elegance of the meal by holding a distinctive name card and flowers. This fold works well with formal or casual, cotton or polyester blend napkins.

Choose the right fold for the occasion. The Tri-Fold, with its double compartments, is perfect to hold utensils and a moist towelette for picnics or barbeques.

1. Place the napkin flat on the table with the wrong side facing up and form a rectangle (p9) by bringing the bottom edge up two-thirds of the way to the top and bringing the top edge down to the bottom folded edge.

2. Turn over a 2 to 3 inch hem on each side.

3. Now fold the left edge to just cover the open edges of the hem on the right side.

4. Fold the left edge again to the right about two-thirds of the way so that the folded edges are equidistant. Use this napkin empty or filled, and place it vertically or horizontally.

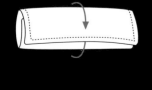

1

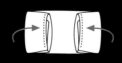

2

3

4

TRUE TRIANGLE

The true triangle is an awesome shape to tuck under the corner of a saucer or even stand up against a cup or glass. It looks like a clown hat and is easy to fold from starched napkins.

1. Fold a one-third rectangle (p9). Hold your finger on the upper right corner and fold the lower right corner to a point midway up the rectangle.

2. Fold the upper right corner down to the bottom edge along the half line made by the last fold.

NOTE The edge of the resulting triangle should lie directly over the rectangle's bottom edge. All corners should point nicely. If they do not, re-do steps 1 and 2 until they are nicely pointed.

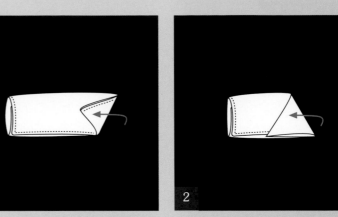

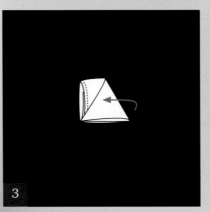

3. Fold this triangle over to the left again along the left edge of the triangle. Again, sharpen the corner points. Repeat. End at the lower left corner of the rectangle.

4. This new triangle has an opening at the left edge. Tuck the remains of the rectangle into this pocket. Straighten any floppy corners.

LOVE-ME KNOT

Not only does this fold resemble a tie, the folding process will seem similar as well. This design looks best sitting on the plate, but care must be taken to keep it in top shape.

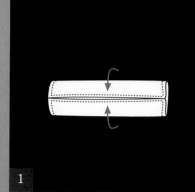

NOTE Use a large napkin. You may have to refold the last folds so do not finger press folds until you are satisfied with the finished look.

1. Begin with a rectangle (p9) made by bringing the lower edge to the top. Then fold the top and bottom edges into the imaginary center line.

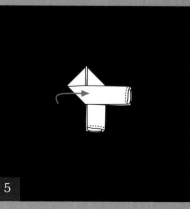

2. Fold the bottom edge to the top to complete the rectangle.

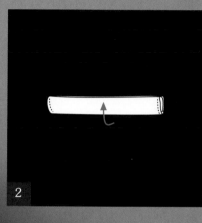

3. Fold the right edge at a right angle down and over the rectangle. At this stage you may need to fold and refold a few times to get the proper finished look.

4. Fold the left edge at a right angle down and over so that the center lines are even and you have a triangle at the top.

NOTE If the left edge is longer by approximately the width of the rectangle, this is correct.

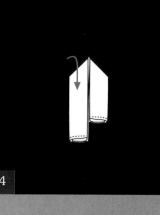

5. Then fold the left side UP and ACROSS the right side at a right angle. Turn the Love-Me Knot for any number of looks.

CHAPTER THREE

❧

Basic
folds from triangles

Triangles have three sides and angles. These napkin folds
offer possibilities for great experimenting.

*A*LL the folds pictured here begin by folding the napkin
into a basic triangle in various ways. Many of these
are folded with the same steps used in the squares
and rectangles done previously.

SHAWL

This graceful triangle fold napkin design is a quarterfold triangle with a quick flip. It is easy and quick to do.

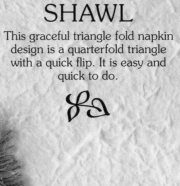

1. Place the napkin flat on the table and make a basic quarter triangle fold (p10). Be sure the open corners are at the lower left.

2. Flip the open corners over to the right. They can be staggered for a more shawl-like effect.

HANKY

This is another fold that enhances napkins with border designs. It works well with softer, cotton-poly blend napkins. Though a very sleek and simple design, it is impressive enough for even the most formal affair.

1. Fold the napkin in half diagonally from left to right to form a half triangle (p10).

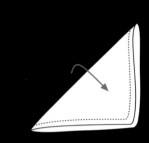

2. Fold the bottom corner up to a point slightly to the right of the top point.

3. Again, fold the bottom corner up to a point slightly to the right of this second top point.

NOTE You may need to roll this fold under a little to get a good point on top.

FORTUNE COOKIE

This classic fold is known by many names. It is used by some oriental restaurants to hold chopsticks for each patron. It looks particularly striking using a gold striped napkin.

1. Place the napkin flat on the table and fold it in half so that the fold is at the top.

2. Fold the top right corner down to the bottom point. Repeat with the top left corner.

3. Flip the napkin over, keeping the open corners at the bottom. Bring the top corner down to the bottom point.

4. Lifting up the napkin by the center point, place left and right corners to the back, to resemble a fortune cookie.

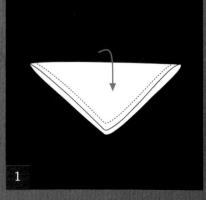

1

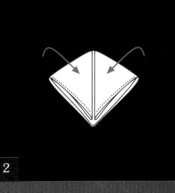

2

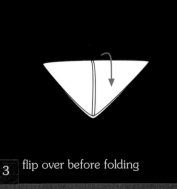

3 flip over before folding

4

TULIP

The petals of this spring napkin flower can be widened as much as you like. As the flower opens, the bottom point becomes more of a "U" shape, resembling a tulip. An array of these in bright yellows, red, and blues brightens any table.

1. Complete steps 1 and 2 of Fortune Cookie (p33). Rotate the napkin so that the open edges are at the top.

2. Fold in the right edge so it lines up with the center line, making a right triangle. Repeat with the left side.

3. Fold the napkin in half to the OUTSIDE. (You will have to pick up the napkin to do this.) Then set the napkin down on the medium length side and let the folds fall so they lie flat. You may need to push the middle fold down to help it divide evenly.

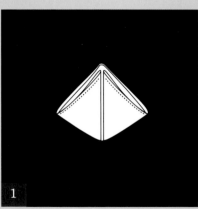

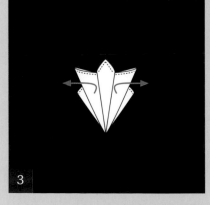

NOTE If you do not like how it looks, pick the napkin up again into its folds and lay it down again.

When you slip the point of Tulip into a napkin ring and spread out the petals, it becomes Flora. The pink outline in the fold in the photo is accomplished by using two napkins, one slightly smaller than the other. Lay the smaller napkin under the larger with the right sides facing the table. Then fold them as one napkin and slide them into a napkin ring.

ENVELOPE

Perfect envelopes start from perfect squares. As long as the napkin is square, the fabric doesn't matter. Cloth or paper, cotton or polyester will make a great design, although polyester may require pressing the last few folds. Since you don't want to overpower the plate, choose smaller napkins – 16 inches or less.

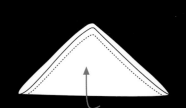

1. Fold the napkin in half diagonally so that the long side is at the bottom.

2. Keeping the bottom edges even, fold the right corner to the left, two-thirds the way across. DO NOT finger press this edge. Fold the left side over to the right edge. You may need to refold the last step if your two-thirds measurement was not precise. Then you can finger press both sides.

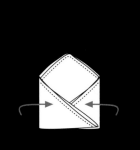

3. Take the point of the top layer (it will be the bottom right corner) and fold it back to the left bottom corner, forming a very small triangle.

4. Open this small triangle into a tiny square.

NOTE Hold the top corner in place with a finger and bring the left corner back toward the right. When it is standing straight up, push it open and down to meet the point your finger is holding. Make the edges even if needed.

5. Fold the napkin in half, bringing the top point down to the bottom point of the small square. To finish, tuck the point into the small square.

NOTE Since part of the folded edges will also be included in this fold, hold the bottom half with your fully opened hand. This helps to establish the fold line and also helps to keep the corners crisp. Add a place card or after dinner mint if you wish.

TRISTE

Use this design to hold breadsticks, silverware, sticks of candy, a flower, or a party favor. For a business luncheon, set the napkin atop a small legal pad and put a gift pen in the knot. Paper does not work well here. Choose cloth – polyester is great.

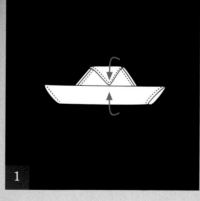

1. Fold the napkin in half diagonally forming a triangle with the long edge at the bottom. Fold in both the top and bottom toward the middle so that they meet at the imaginary center point.

2. Bring the small half over the larger to form a strip.

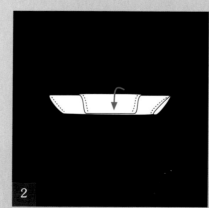

3. Knot this strip loosely in the middle.

NOTE Flip the right edge up and then the left, leaving an inch or two of the bottom edge in place. Bring your right hand through that bottom edge and pull the top edge through for the knot. Keep this knot loose and adjust it to sit nicely.

FOUR POINTS

This design has a striking geometric shape that lends itself to a tailored table setting. There are no open edges in this very compact design.

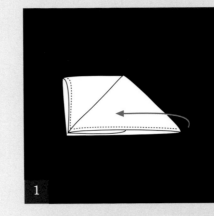

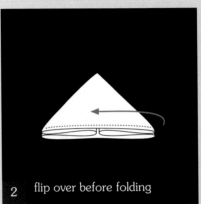

1. The starting triangle comes from the quarterfold square (p9). Be sure that the open edges are at the bottom and the folded edge at the top. Hold your finger on the upper middle and bring only the top layer of the bottom right corner over to the left. This opens the square out into a large triangle.

2. Flip the napkin over. The square side should be at the right. Repeat, again bringing the top layer of the bottom right corner over to the left.

NOTE Hold the left triangle in place and make the new triangle match it. Be sure the center lines of the folds underneath this large triangle meet.

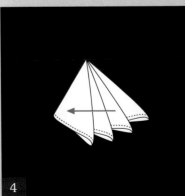

2 flip over before folding

3. Fold this large triangle in half from left to right. You now have four triangles.

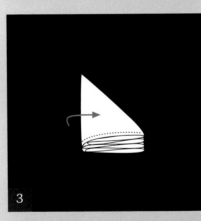

3

4. Hold the top point and fan out the four triangles.

4

CHAPTER FOUR

❦

Rolled napkins

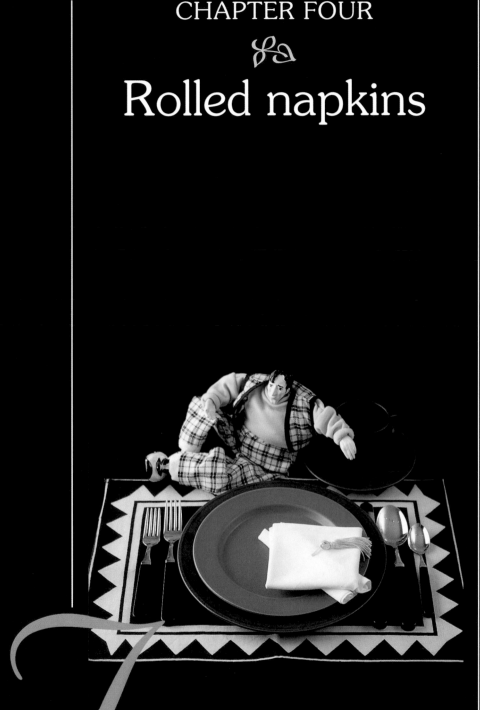

*T*HESE are decorative napkins made by various methods of rolling. Since many of these will not lie properly on the plate or table without unrolling, they are finished by placing them in a glass or napkin ring.

ROLL

The simplest of all, the basic roll can grace any spot on your table setting.

❧

1. Place the napkin flat on the table and fold it in half to form a rectangle (p9). Begin at one end and roll the napkin.

2. Roll all the way across. Depending on the fabric, the napkin may or may not need to be held in a ring. However, a ring is always a welcome decorating extra.

NOTE All napkin rings do not have the same size opening. You may need to roll your napkin tighter or more loosely to fit the ring.

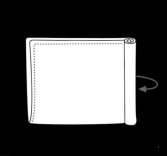

VARIATIONS

a) Start with a rectangle made from thirds (p9). This eliminates the open edge. Fold the napkin evenly in thirds or turn both edges down several inches. Then roll. This finished roll can be any width you determine.

b) Roll two napkins of contrasting colors.

c) Combine these two variations. Fold one napkin in half. Lay a contrasting napkin on top and turn its edges in so that an inch or two overlaps the bottom napkin. Now roll them both together.

d) Try rolling a square or triangle.

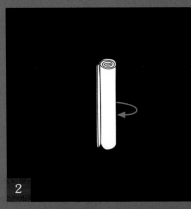

A roll with a purpose is the Diploma. It is a simple design, but it can be used for formal occasions. Use paper or cloth. Tie it with a ribbon or a flower ornament.

1. Fold the napkin in half to form a rectangle (p9). Roll one end of the napkin tightly about two-thirds the way across the rectangle. Hold the roll with one hand and turn down the top corner of the open edge at the midpoint. Repeat, but this time hold the fold and the roll with one hand and fold up the bottom corner of the open edge at the midpoint to complete the triangle.

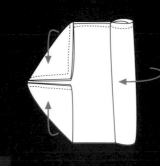

1

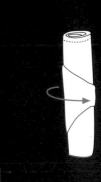

2

CURTAINS

This is a charming design made more dramatic by using two contrasting napkins – a print and a solid. Leave it straight or pull each side apart slightly at the bottom to resemble open window curtains.

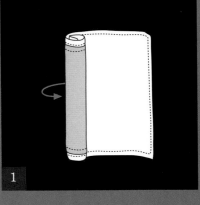

1. Use two contrasting napkins, each of a different size. For the effect pictured here, the print napkin should be smaller than the plain one. Lay the larger napkin on the table with the smaller napkin centered on top of it with the right sides facing up. Then flip the pair over. Begin to roll one side.

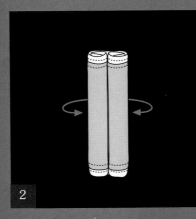

2. Roll in BIG, LOOSE rolls to the center. Roll in the opposite side to the center, also in BIG, LOOSE rolls. Adjust the rolls so they look even in width.

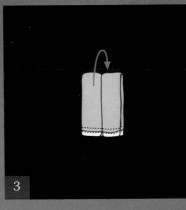

3. Finger press the rolls flat and fold the top half of the napkin underneath and to the back. Spread out the bottom edges.

NOTE If you fold just slightly less than half to the back, the front will overlap and have a neater edge.

MIDDLE ROLL

The Middle Roll adds wonderful dimension to what appears to be a normal rectangular dinner napkin. Use two napkins the same size for the best results. Even the wildest choices of colors and prints combine beautifully in this design.

1. Lay two napkins on top of each other making sure the bottom edges are even. For print, the wrong sides should face each other. Fold the right edge of the double napkin to the imaginary center line.

2. Now fold the left edge along this same center line so that it completely overlaps the right side.

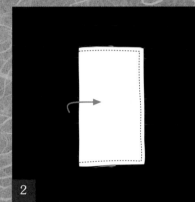

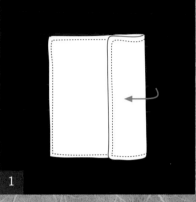

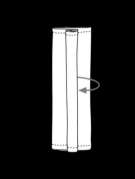

3. Roll this new right edge back toward the left until you have a roll in the center of the bottom layer.

4. Flatten this roll and fold the top half of the napkin to the back and underneath the finished design.

LICORICE STICK

This fold is a contender for two prizes. It is a sure favorite in the most-fun-to-fold category and a pleasing choice in the most-dramatic-effect-produced category. Use two napkins that are square and the same size – either cloth or paper.

1. Lay one napkin flat on the table diagonally with the wrong side facing up. Lay a second napkin on top of it also with the wrong side facing up. Leave about a 1 inch frame of the underneath napkin showing on the two bottom edges.

2. Starting at the bottom corner, roll the napkins together all the way to the top.

3. Fold the roll in half and insert into a glass.

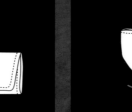

1. Start with a rectangle formed by folding the napkin in thirds (p9).

2. Fold the right and left edges up from the bottom center point at a right angle.

1

2

Every graduation deserves a special napkin on the plate. Place a simple tassel from a fabric store on the completed napkin for emphasis. Try a combination of Diploma folds (p41) and Graduation Cap folds for your table setting.

3   flip over before folding

3. Hold the bottom center point and flip over the napkin. Keep the point of the triangle at the top. Roll up each of the rectangular flaps TIGHTLY to just over the triangle.

NOTE Hold the first roll down with a cup or saucer while you roll the second.

to begin with, roll is underneath at top edge

4   flip over before folding

4. Holding the rolls, flip the napkin over so that the rolls are underneath at the top edge. Fold the roll on the right side down to the center so that the roll ends up on top and lines up with the center line. Repeat with the roll on the left.

5. Flip the napkin over and press it down firmly so that the square lies neatly on the rolls.

5   flip over before pressing

CANDLES

These Candles are perfect for fringed and less than square napkins. They are made easily from any type of fabric, but paper won't survive the handling.

1. Fold the napkin in half forming a triangle with the folded edge at the bottom.

2. Fold the top point down, almost to the bottom edge.

3. Fold the napkin in half again by bringing the top edge down to the bottom edge to form a strip. Then fold the left edge of the strip up at a right angle along the line formed by the top layer of the strip.

4. Leaving the "wick" exposed, roll the strip tightly from left to right. Tuck the bottom corner of the diagonal edge of the strip under a layer of the roll at the bottom edge.

5. Stand the candle up.

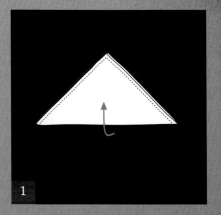

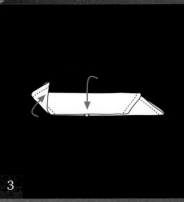

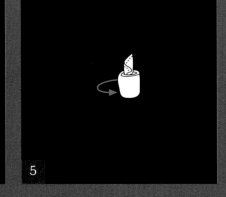

CANDELABRA

The Candelabra is an extravagant fold and needs a napkin ring to stand. While not particularly a no-fuss fold, it is an example of what can be accomplished from combining folding techniques.

4. Holding this roll, begin accordion pleating (p10) the rest of the way down the napkin. This may look sloppy, but will look fine in the end.

5. Fold in half with the rolls in the middle and the pleats on the outside. Stand this up in a napkin ring. The pleats will flare out.

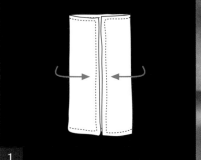

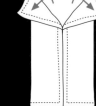

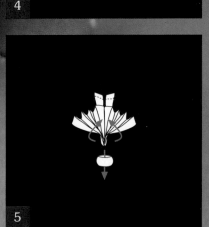

1. Form a rectangle by folding both the left and right edges into an imaginary center line.

2. Fold the top corners out and over the edges forming triangles that resemble an open shirt collar.

NOTE Iron these folds to help hold them in place during the upcoming rolling and pleating.

3. Roll the top edge down to the bottom point of this open section.

CHAPTER FIVE

Accordion pleated folds

*R*EMEMBER the first time you accordion pleated a piece of paper in school to make a fan? Accordion pleating cloth napkins can be just as much fun.

BASIC FLOWER

The Basic Flower is a common fold, yet timeless in its beauty. It is easy to do and works well with polyester napkins.

1. Lay the napkin flat. Accordion fold (p10) the entire napkin.

2. Fold this pleated strip in half and slip the folded end into a napkin ring and flare out the folds.

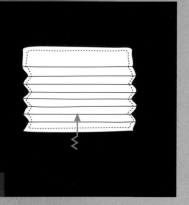

BASIC FAN

By using two napkins of different sizes you can accentuate the pleats with a border hem. If using one napkin, try leaving a little of the bottom half showing to achieve the same result.

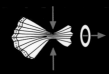

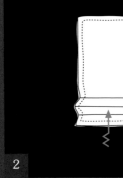

1. Fold the napkin in half from right to left. (You can leave some of the edge of the bottom napkin showing.)

2. Accordion pleat (p10) the entire napkin.

3. Slip the folded edge into a napkin ring.

FARFALLE

In this variation, the folded napkin is set on a bordered napkin and both are accordion pleated as one.

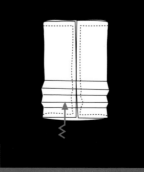

1. Fold both right and left edges to the imaginary center line to form a rectangle.

2. Accordion pleat (p10) the entire napkin from the bottom up.

3. Slide the napkin ring onto the pleated strip all the way to the middle. Spread out the folds.

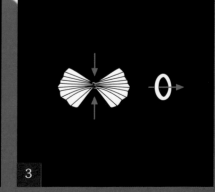

MINISKIRT

To create this design, fold a 10 inch napkin in half, then accordion pleat (p10). This time put the open ends into a napkin ring and flare the folds.

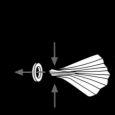

1. Start with the Basic Fan using one napkin. Insert the open edges of the napkin into a napkin ring so that the ring hides the edges. Flair out the folds to resemble a skirt.

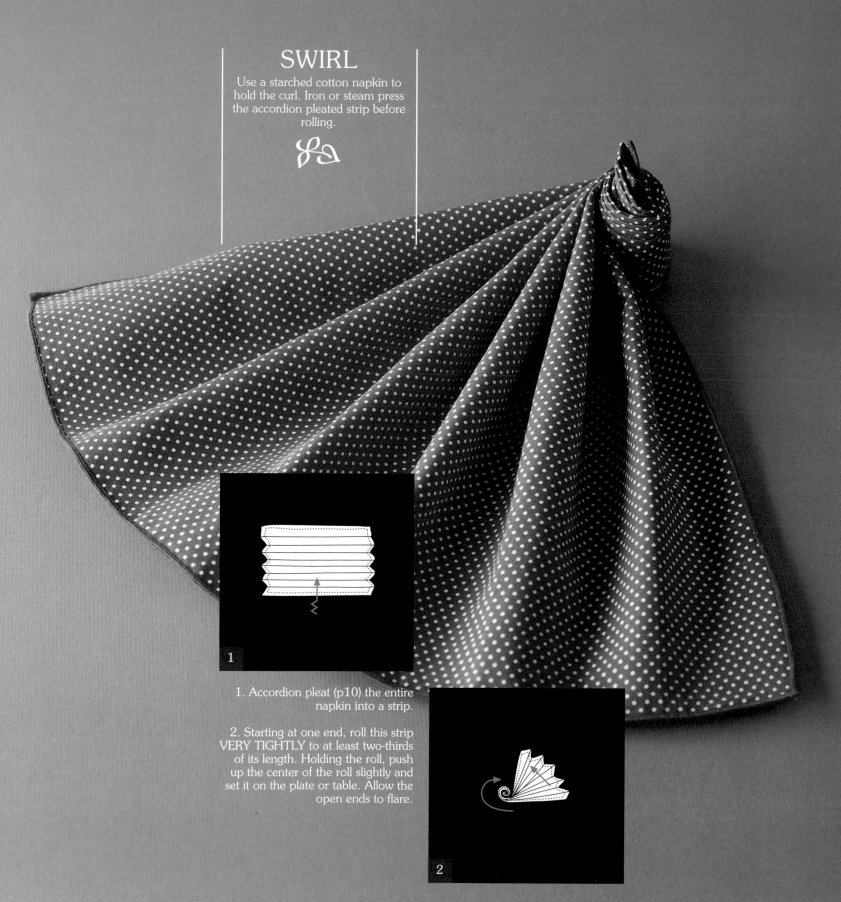

SWIRL

Use a starched cotton napkin to hold the curl. Iron or steam press the accordion pleated strip before rolling.

1. Accordion pleat (p10) the entire napkin into a strip.

2. Starting at one end, roll this strip VERY TIGHTLY to at least two-thirds of its length. Holding the roll, push up the center of the roll slightly and set it on the plate or table. Allow the open ends to flare.

This fold is a progression from the basic triangle fold (p10). It is wonderfully versatile and can stand up in a napkin ring or cup.

1. Start with a half triangle (p10) with the folded edge at the bottom. Then fold the bottom edge up two-thirds of the way toward the top corner.

2. Starting at the left side, accordion pleat (p10) the napkin to the center line. Flip the napkin over and continue pleating to the end.

NOTE Be sure the beginning pleat and the ending pleat are pointing in the same direction. They may even extend past the folds.

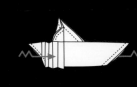

3. Stand the folded napkin up in a napkin ring and pull the bottom corner points down. Sit the napkin on a plate or in a glass.

NOTE Either the plain or the pleated side can be displayed as the correct finished side of this design. Both are considered proper.

IRIS

This beautiful flower shape formed by accordion pleating (p10) is best displayed in a goblet or wine glass. Use ornate damask cloth napkins. Polyester blend can be used, but gives a softer look.

5. Insert into a glass or napkin ring.

1. Start with a half triangle (p9) with the folded edge at the bottom.

2. Fold the left and right sides up to the center point. Holding the bottom corner, spread the top out a couple of inches.

3. Fold the bottom corner up two-thirds of the way toward the top corner point.

4. Starting at the left side, accordion pleat (p10) the entire length of the napkin.

NOTE This will be easier to do if you turn the napkin sideways first and pleat from the bottom to the top.

CENTER RUFFLE

This unusual design makes a delightfully animated Center Ruffle. Any fabric works and two contrasting napkins result in an especially distinctive design.

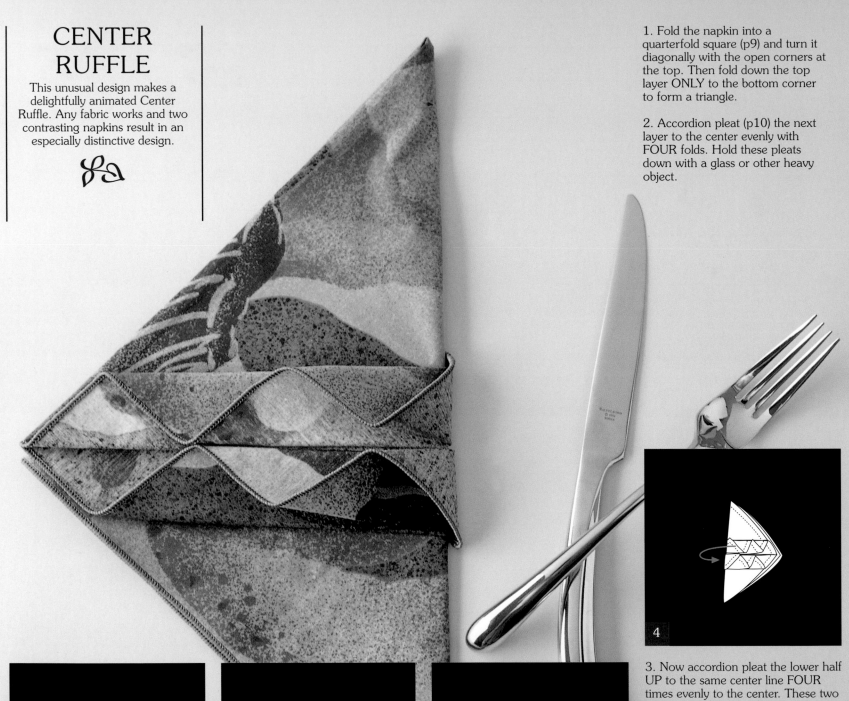

1. Fold the napkin into a quarterfold square (p9) and turn it diagonally with the open corners at the top. Then fold down the top layer ONLY to the bottom corner to form a triangle.

2. Accordion pleat (p10) the next layer to the center evenly with FOUR folds. Hold these pleats down with a glass or other heavy object.

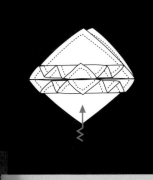

3. Now accordion pleat the lower half UP to the same center line FOUR times evenly to the center. These two rows of accordion pleats should now be mirror images.

4. Holding the center pleats, pick up the right sides of the napkin and flip the left side underneath it to fold the napkin in half so that the ruffles are on the outside.

NOTE The center ruffle can be turned in any direction to adorn your table.

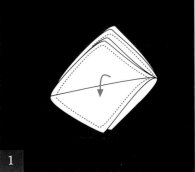

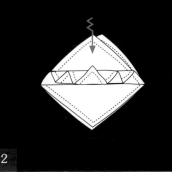

CHAPTER SIX

❧

Folds for
napkin rings

Napkin rings can also be used with the following designs: Scarf p23,
Flora p35, Roll p40, Candelabra p47, Basic Fan p50, Farfalle p51,
Miniskirt p52, Fleur p54, Bow p66, Yesterday p75,
Victorian p76, and Obelisk p83.

D O you have napkin rings to display? These folds are
a perfect complement to your heirloom or
collectible napkin holders.

DAINTY PULL

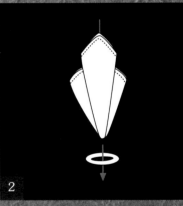

1. Make a quarterfold square (p9).

2. Pull the folded corner through a napkin ring. This is a simple and quick way to show off embroidered napkins and elegant napkin rings.

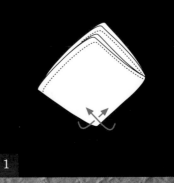

BOUQUET

1. Place the napkin flat on the table. Fold the bottom right corner up over the midpoint of the top line forming three triangles of equal size.

2. Pull the napkin through the ring at the center point of the bottom fold line.

DOUBLE BOUQUET

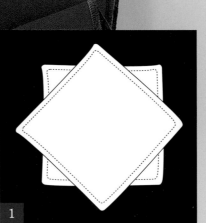

1. Lay one napkin flat on the table in a square. Lay the second napkin on top in a diamond shape.

2. Pick up both napkins by the very center point and slip them through a napkin ring.

SHOOTING STAR

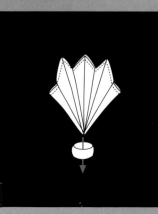

1. Start by making the Tulip (p34). Slip the bottom point into a napkin ring.

CONE

This fold retains its geometric shape when pulled through a ring and looks great in large napkin holders. The Cone is suitable for any table decor and can be fashioned using cloth or paper napkins.

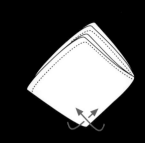

1. Fold the napkin into a quarterfold square (p9) and turn it diagonally with the open corners at the top.

2. Fold the right side to the left two-thirds of the way across. Be sure to keep a sharp point at the bottom.

3. Fold the left side over this right edge, keeping a sharp point at the bottom. The napkin will now resemble a cone.

4. Slide the napkin ring over the point, flip over and adjust the fullness.

2

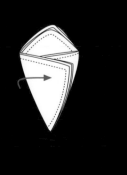

3

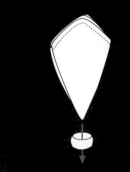

4

BOW TIE

The Bow Tie is a classic napkin fold. It can be produced from any size napkin in the fabric of your choice.

1. Start with a quarterfold square (p9). Turn it diagonally with the folded corner at the bottom.

2. Starting at the bottom, accordion pleat (p10) the napkin evenly up to the top corner. Since you are working with 4 layers of fabric, you will need to pleat this by turning it over after each fold, at least until you get to the center.

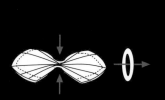

NOTE You need not be concerned with the outer edges while you are pleating since they will be flared eventually. Just be sure the center is even and the ending pleat is folded in the same direction as the beginning pleat.

3. Holding the pleats firmly, insert the napkin into a napkin ring. Fan out the sides until both sides are even.

Napkins into animals and objects

AVE fun with these napkin folds that resemble ordinary objects and favorite animals. Do some with paper and others with finest damask. They look difficult but are actually combinations of basic folds and techniques.

HEART

This fold looks especially attractive
with a scalloped-edge napkin.

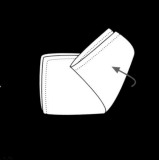

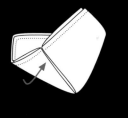

1. Fold the napkin in half so that
the folded edge is at the bottom.
Then fold the right side to the left
two-thirds of the way across. Be sure
to keep a sharp point at the bottom.

2. Fold the left side over this right
edge, keeping a sharp point at the
bottom.

3. Flip the napkin over. It will now
resemble a heart.

BOW

This Bow is easy to master from
steps already learned.

1. Complete steps 1 and 2 of the
Triste (p37).

2. Fold the right end down at an
angle.

3. Fold the left end down at an angle,
leaving about 2 to 3 inches of the top
edge exposed.

4. With your thumb at the bottom
intersection and your index finger at
the top, pinch the napkin together
vertically and hold it firmly. Hang on
with one hand and push one end into
a napkin ring. Straighten the bow.

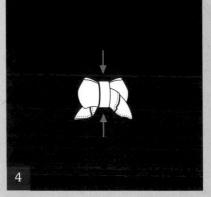

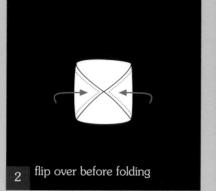

1

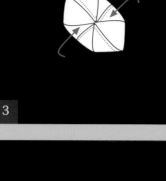

2 flip over before folding

3

1. Lay the napkin on the table diagonally and fold in the top and bottom corners to the center point. (Folding the napkin in quarters and unfolding it will give you an exact center point.)

2. Flip the napkin over carefully and then fold the left and right corners to the center point.

3. Fold the top right and bottom left points into the center point.

4. Holding all center points in place, again flip the napkin over. Fold the remaining two points to the center point.

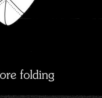

4 flip over before folding

5. Taking the center point of one of the triangles (the square corner of the second layer), pull the fold to open up a larger triangle. Now do the same with the triangle directly opposite.

6. Again, holding the center points firmly, flip the napkin over. Now pull out the center points (the square corner of the second layer) of two remaining triangles to complete the pinwheel.

NOTE The design looks best using a napkin with a design on both sides, or one with solid color on both sides. If you want to really test your skill, try using two contrasting napkins. Keep in mind that they need to be perfectly square.

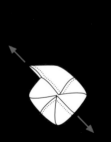

5

6 flip over before pulling

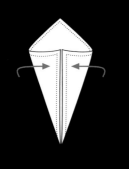

1

2

PEACOCK

This fine bird looks exceptional perched in a goblet at your finest gala. For best results use a large cloth napkin, plenty of starch, and a steam iron.

1. Lay a large napkin flat on the table diagonally with the RIGHT side up. Fold the right and left sides into the imaginary center line. Press this firmly, especially the bottom point. (This will be the head and mouth, so make sure you have a nice point.)

2. Fold the bottom point up to the middle of the horizontal edges of these new triangles. Press firmly. Then fold the point of this new triangle back down, not quite halfway, to form a head. Press very firmly.

NOTE If you are making these ahead of party time, you may want to place a small piece of thin cardboard inside the opening in the back of the section making the body of the bird just below the fold that makes the head. This will keep it from going limp.

5

3. Fold the entire napkin in half lengthwise to the OUTSIDE. Finger press.

4. Grasping the body section firmly, gently pull and fan out the tail section. The body should now be standing upright.

5. Set this in a glass and spread out the tail.

3

4

FISHYTAIL

This design combines two completely different napkin fold designs to make a new one that resembles a fish. Fishytail is made of a bottom triangle (the fish's head) and a top napkin (the fin and tail). The nice thing about this fold is that neatness doesn't count. Edges that do not match perfectly add depth and give movement to the creature.

2. Ruffle. Complete the Center Ruffle (p56), except the final fold in half. Hold on to the ruffles.

3. Make a hexagon by folding the top and bottom corners under and to the back center point.

NOTE For a variation on Fishytail, form the fish's head from a square napkin folded diagonally twice. This makes a triangle that has open edges on the long side. You can then tuck the ruffled napkin inside rather than laying it on the top. If you want even more flamboyance, add yet another color napkin – a smaller triangle for a tail. Or, you can reverse the order so that there is a smaller triangle, ruffle, and then large triangle for the tail.

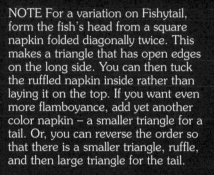

3

4

1. Head. Fold a napkin in quarters and then in half to make a triangle. Set aside.

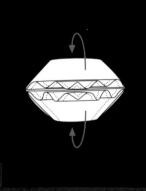

4. Now you can do that last fold. Pick the napkin up slightly, holding the folds and ruffles firmly, and fold it in half so that the ruffles are on the outside.

5. Lay this on the larger triangle.

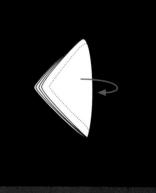

1

2

5

BUTTERFLY

This three-dimensional fold enhances any table. The wings of the Butterfly appear to be fluttering, ready for flight.

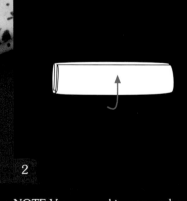

7

6

6. Starting on the right side, take the top layer and bring it to the left, thus opening out the triangle at the bottom. Crease this triangle in place and take the top layer back to its starting point so that the triangle is inside the pleat. This new triangle gives the wing its lift.

7. Repeat step 5 on the left side, bringing the top layer to the right to open up the triangle at the bottom.

5

1

2

1. Fold the top and bottom edges into the imaginary center line.

2. Fold the bottom edge up to the top on the center line to form a strip.

3. Fold the right edge two-thirds of the way across to the left.

4. Then fold it back to the folded edge.

NOTE You are making a very large pleat.

5. Fold the left edge over to the right edge and back again to the left folded edge, again making a large pleat. The napkin should now look like an open book.

3

4

BUNNY

These cute little creatures will hop right onto your place setting. Use a starched cloth napkin and press the folds as you proceed.

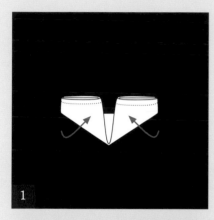

1

2

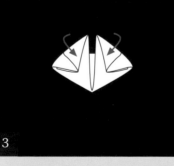

3

5. Holding this fold in place, flip the napkin over again. Tuck the right side into the open triangle at the left just enough to hold it in place while you open it out into a cone shape and stand it up.

6. Spread out the ears and the Bunny is complete.

1. Follow steps 1 to 3 for Graduation Cap (p45).

2. Holding the center point, fold the top right and left edges down to form small triangles.

3. Fold these triangles over to the center fold line. Press if needed.

4. Flip the napkin over. Fold the bottom point up to the horizontal line and back down to form the tail.

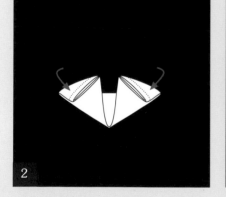

4 flip over before folding

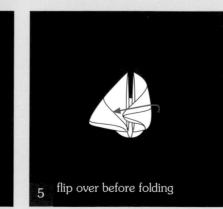

5 flip over before folding

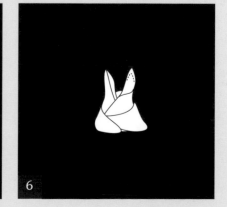

6

BOAT

These Boats are perfect for a Bon Voyage party or any children's festivities. You can use paper, but very stiff cloth napkins work best.

1. Lay napkin flat and make a quarterfold square (p9). Turn it so that the folded corner is at the TOP.

2. Fold the bottom point of the top THREE layers to the top folded corner point.

3. Flip the napkin over and fold the remaining single layer up to the top point from this side.

4. Turn up a small hem (an inch or two) all the way around the bottom long edge of the triangle. Separate the bottom edges slightly to help the center triangle stand up.

NOTE The corners are vital to the hem. Try turning up the center of the hem on the front and back. Then, while holding this in place, poke your thumb into the side corners to help them turn and point upright.

1

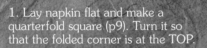

2

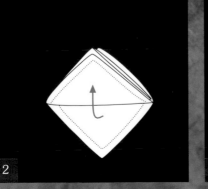

3   flip over before folding

BANANA SPLIT

These napkin designs can be
especially fun with little candies
hidden inside.

1. Make the Boat (p72).

2. Roll the single layers of the middle
triangles down and tuck them into the
body of the boat.

NOTE Roll the folded layer last.

Folds to show off napkins

*U*SE these fold designs to display fine embroidered or fancy napkins or special heirloom pieces.

YESTERDAY

Use this fold to show off delicately edged napkins or special heirloom pieces.

1. Start with the quarterfold square (p9). Turn it diagonally so the open corners are at the top.

2. Fold in the left and right corners to the imaginary center point.

1

2

3

4

3. Fold in these left and right sides to the imaginary center line.

4. Fold the napkin vertically in half along the center line.

5

5. Turn the napkin over and slip on a napkin ring. Flare out the napkin.

VARIATION
At step 4 you can fold the napkin in half to the OUTSIDE instead.

VICTORIAN

Use this fold to display intricately embroidered napkins.

3. Turn the napkin over and slip on a napkin ring. You may need to spread the edges of the top slightly.

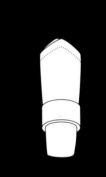

1. Complete steps 1 and 2 of Yesterday (p75). Then fold the bottom corner up to the imaginary center.

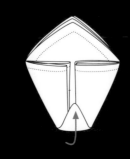

2. Fold the right edge to the left about two-thirds of the way. Then fold the left edge over the right.

HANDKERCHIEF

Handkerchief is a perfect way to display napkins with corner embroidery, lace, or heirloom monograms. This tailored design is suitable for dinner or luncheon settings.

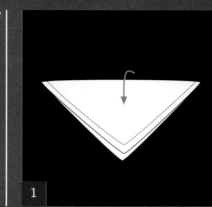

1. Lay the napkin flat on the table diagonally with the monogram or design at the bottom corner, right side down, facing the table. Fold the top corner down to the bottom point.

2. Fold the left corner to the bottom point and the right corner to the bottom point.

3. Bring the left corner to the center fold so that the left edge is lined up with the center fold line. Fold the right corner to the center in the same fashion.

4. Flip the napkin over while firmly holding all the corners. Fold the bottom point to the back to form a base.

NOTE If you would like this napkin to sit at a more elevated angle, add one more fold. After turning the bottom point back (step 4), fold that edge one more time back up to the top. You will have to crease this very heavily to keep it from unfolding, but it makes a nice stand to display the design.

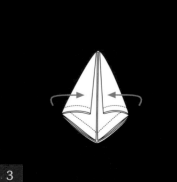

COURTESY

This fold nicely displays a bordered napkin.

1. Follow steps 1 to 5 of Four Points (p38). Then pick up the folded napkin by the point and set it on the table or plate. Open the bottom points to help it stand upright.

PROPPED FAN

Do not be intimidated by the grandeur of this show piece. A few folds, some rolling, and accordion pleating make this design easy to do. It is ideally suited for large, extravagant, and lavish print napkins.

2. Accordion pleat (p10) the napkin from the bottom two-thirds of the way to the top edge. The first accordion fold should be toward the back.

3. Flip the accordion folds underneath the napkin so they are at the bottom edge. Then fold the entire napkin in half from right to left. Be sure the accordion folds are on the outside and the open edges are at the left.

4. Fold down the top edge to form a small hem (about one inch).

5. Fold the left edge of the top hem at an angle and tuck it under the bottom right corner of the accordion fold. This makes the stand.

6. Pick the napkin up from the left by the accordion folds so that it is sitting on this stand. Let go of the folds and the fan will open. Center the folds.

1

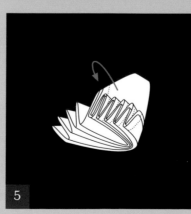

2

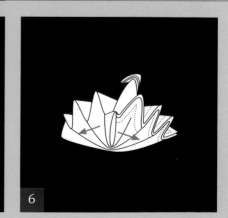

3

1. Lay the napkin on the table with the wrong side up and fold the left edge to the right side, forming a rectangle.

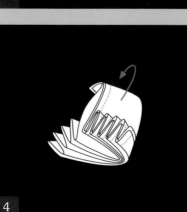

4

5

6

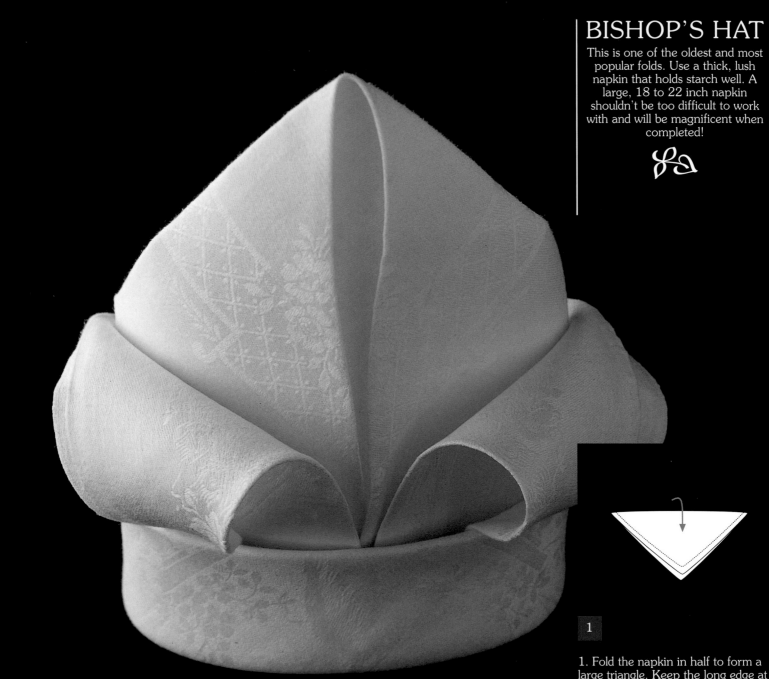

This is one of the oldest and most popular folds. Use a thick, lush napkin that holds starch well. A large, 18 to 22 inch napkin shouldn't be too difficult to work with and will be magnificent when completed!

1

1. Fold the napkin in half to form a large triangle. Keep the long edge at the top.

3

3. Fold these same left and right triangles back up to the top center point.

2

2. Fold the right edge down along the center line. Now fold the left edge down along this same center line.

4. To form the band, take both layers at the bottom corner and fold them up to the middle point of the center fold line made by the previous step.

5. Fold the bottom edge up to this same point.

4

5

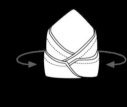

7

6

7. Flip the napkin over so that the point is at the top. Fold the left and right corners in toward each other and tuck the right corner into the band of the left.

6. Once again, fold the bottom edge up, this time along the center fold line so that it forms a band resting on the triangles.

8

8. Set the napkin upright with the band at the bottom. Round out the shape. Then tuck the right and left triangles into the band, as shown.

VARIATIONS
Leave the triangles out for a wing-like effect or pull the triangles all the way down to the band to resemble a collar.

TRI-PETALS

Tri-Petals is a wonderful choice for displaying your most intricately embellished napkins. This delicate flower shape is elegant for weddings or a summer garden party.

1. Follow steps 1 and 2 of Bishop's Hat (p80). The embellished design should show on the bottom point of the first large triangle.

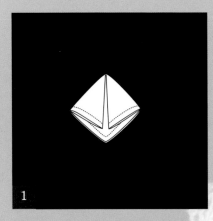

2. Flip the napkin over. Fold all the bottom corners up to the top point making a smaller triangle. Flip the napkin over.

3. Fold the left and right corners in toward each other.

4. Tuck one of the corners into the open edges of the other corner. Stand napkin upright on folded edge and round out the shape.

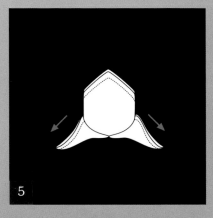

5. Turn napkin so tucked folded edges are at the back. Peel down the side triangles until they lie nicely on the table, revealing the embellished design.

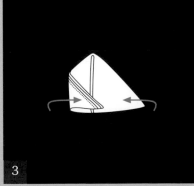

OBELISK

A napkin ring that will sit on the table and hold a napkin upright is a prerequisite for this design.

1. Fold the napkin to form a large triangle with the napkin's design in the center.

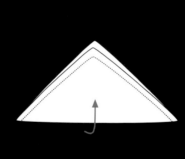

1

2. Fold the long bottom edge up to form a band just a bit wider than the napkin ring.

2

3 flip over before rolling

3. Flip the napkin over. Roll the left side into the center and then the right side into the center.

4. Set it in a napkin ring. Spread out the top point.

4

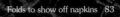

CHAPTER NINE

❧

Napkin folds
that hold
things

*T*HESE decorative napkins serve dual duty. They not
only beautify the table, but also hold items of
importance for hostess and diner. Silverware, flowers,
trinkets, crayons, even gifts can be tucked inside
these folds. This design is ideal for buffets, since the
guest can pick up the napkin and flatware all at once.

POCKET

Hide a surprise for your guest in this Pocket design napkin.

1. Start with a quarterfold square (p9) and place it diagonally on the table with open corners at the top.

2. Fold the left, right, and bottom corners in to the imaginary center point.

3. Flip the napkin over and fold one or two of the top layers down for the flap.

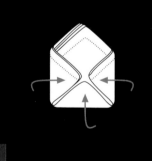

flip over before folding

2. Fold the left and right sides to the back and underneath the napkin. This may be easier if you flip the napkin over first.

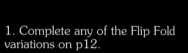

1. Complete any of the Flip Fold variations on p12.

2

1

FLATWARE FOLD

The technique of simple folding is used for this elegant design. Choose cloth napkins for a more finished look.

1. Lay napkin on the table right side up, then fold in half to make a rectangle with the folded edge at the bottom. Turn the top edge of the top layer back down to the bottom folded edge.

VARIATION Fold the top layer down again to the bottom edge, making a smaller band to show off your silverware.

2. Flip the napkin over. Fold the right edge over to the imaginary center line.

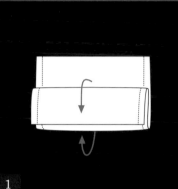

1

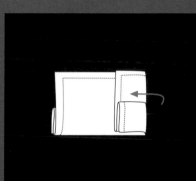

2 flip over before folding

3. Fold the right edge over again, this time folding on the center line.

4. Fold the right edge over again to finish the design.

3

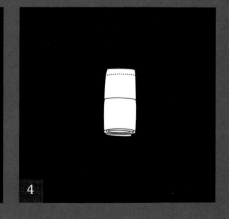

4

CUFFED FLATWARE FOLD

Use two napkins of contrasting color. In step 2, of Flatware Fold (p87), instead of folding the top layer down to the bottom edge, roll the top layer to the middle to make a band. Flip over and continue with the remaining steps.

DIAGONAL CUFF

The trim lines of these Diagonals make striking holders for many table settings.

1. Make a quarterfold square (p9) with the open corners at the upper right. Then roll the top corner ONLY of the first open layer, down to the center and flatten the roll slightly to form a band.

2. Fold the left and right edges under and to the back imaginary center line. Flipping the napkin over first may make this easier to do.

1

2

VARIATIONS

a) Double Diagonal Cuff
Repeat step 1 above. Then fold the next top open layer down and tuck the corner point underneath the roll until a second band is formed of about the same width. Finish the same as above.

b) Triple Diagonal Cuff
Repeat step 1 above. Tuck the corner of the third layer underneath the second band to form a third. Finish the same as above.

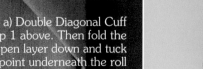

HEXAGON FLATWARE FOLDS

These handy tuck-ins make an exquisite frame for a flower and call attention to fancy flatware. Place napkins on the plate or at its side.

VARIATION
Triple Hexagon Flatware Fold
After rolling the first layer (see below), tuck the corners of the second and third layers underneath the band to form three rolls, as in the Triple Diagonal Cuff (p89). Finish as below.

NOTE If using two napkins, you can roll either the top layer or the top two layers, depending on which color you want for the rolled bands.

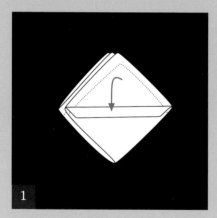

1. Begin with a quarterfold square (p9). Turn it diagonally so that the open corners are at the top. Then roll the top corner ONLY of the first of the four layers down to the center line. Flatten this roll.

flip over before folding

2. Flip the napkin over, keeping it at a diagonal. Fold the right corner to reach two-thirds of the way to the left corner.

3. Bring the left corner over this fold so that it almost reaches the right edge.

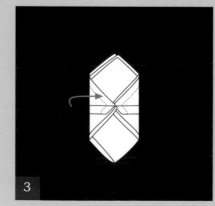

4. Flip the napkin over again and pull out the top edges of the folds slightly to give it an even shape.

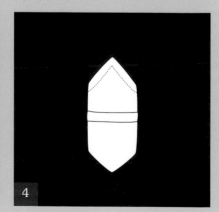

PEEK-A-BOO

Peek-A-Boo forms a perfect spot to hide any small item – perhaps a piece of fine jewelry such as an engagement or anniversary ring?

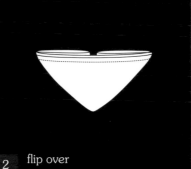

2. Holding the middle of this bottom edge, flip the napkin over so that the long open edge is at the top.

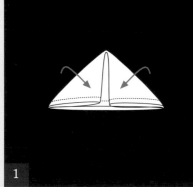

1. Fold the napkin into a half rectangle (p9) with the folded edge at the top. With your finger at the center top point, bring the right and left top corners down to the middle of the bottom edge to form a large triangle.

3. Again, hold your finger at the center top point and bring the right and left top corners down to the middle of the bottom point.

4. Flip the napkin over and fill the center opening.

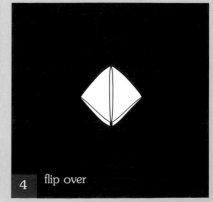

BUN BASKET

This impressive design can be used for each guest or the napkins can be grouped together as a serving piece. Make them up ahead of time and stack them unopened so they will be well pressed or press the folds as you proceed. Use a large cloth napkin and plenty of starch.

1. Fold the napkin into thirds (p9) to form a rectangle.

3. Now fold the right edge and this new left edge to the imaginary center line.

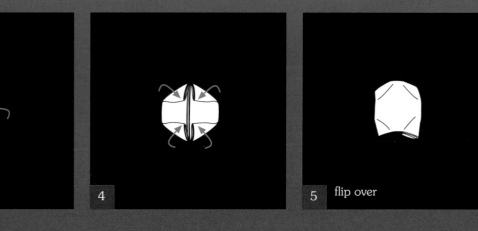

4. Fold down the top left and right corners along the center line to form triangles. PRESS these firmly and then let them go. Repeat for the bottom two corners.

5. With the four corner folds open, flip the napkin over. The four pressed diagonal fold lines across the corners should show.

5   flip over

2. Fold the left side over to the right so that the folded edge is on the left.

6. Pick up the center of the top two layers of the bottom edge and bring them up to the center of the napkin while at the same time pushing the sides towards the middle. This should fold easily on the corner fold lines and form a diamond. Flatten the diamond and press.

8. Flip the napkin over. Pick up the left and right open edges and gently pull them open while at the same time bending the center, horizontal band upwards. Spread out the open edges to form the double basket. Fill immediately.

NOTE At step 8 you can fold the napkin in half to the OUTSIDE. Press and store the napkins this way. When ready to use spread out the open edges.

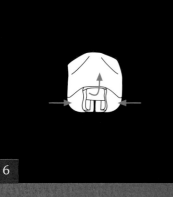

7. Repeat step 6 with the top edge. This diamond overlaps the bottom one.

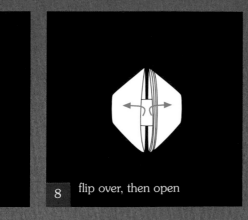

8   flip over, then open

TAKE CARE
OF YOUR NAPKINS

Napkins will get soiled and stained. Knowing how to care for them will put your mind at ease while dining and entertaining.

LAUNDRY TIPS

Cloth napkins require extra care. Vintage linens should always be hand washed. If they are stained, soak them in a non-chlorine bleach set in direct sunlight. They should be stirred and gently swished, not scrubbed. Use a mild detergent. Never wring them. Instead, roll them in a towel until most of the water is absorbed and hang them to dry.

Other fabric napkins will do quite well in your washing machine and even emerge from your dryer needing little or no ironing. A little spray of laundry stain remover as a pre-treatment should restore them for normal use. For tougher stains consult the stain chart (p95).

Whether laundering your napkins by hand or machine, the key to success is in getting them into water quickly. I use my dishwasher and a small mesh laundry bag that holds 4 or 5 napkins. Tie it firmly to the upper rack in your dishwasher, and you can clean the dishes and the napkins all at once immediately following the meal. I recommend this for napkins that can withstand very hot water. Never combine colors and white in the same bag. You can iron them dry or let them hang dry. This method is only for napkins that do not need a chemical stain treatment (since some are poisonous) and you do not want that in your dishwasher.

NAPKIN STORAGE

Store your napkins flat, if possible. For larger 22 inch squares, place them in a suitcase kept under a bed. You can store them pre-folded in basic starting shapes. Another option is to roll the set of napkins before storing.

STAIN TREATMENT

NOTE Stain treatment may not work on all fabrics.

Stain	Pre-treatment
Berries	Soak in cold water with vinegar or white wine before washing.
Candle wax	First scrape off what you can with a blunt knife. Then iron the napkin between paper towels until all the wax is absorbed by the towels.
Chocolate	Rinse 15 minutes in cool water, then soak in enzyme pre-soak in warm water before washing.
Coffee	Rinse 15 minutes in cool water, then blot with diluted vinegar, rinse, and launder.
Egg	Soak in cool water with mild detergent, then clean normally.
Fruit	Rinse 15 minutes in cool water, then soak in enzyme pre-soak in warm water before washing.
Gravy	Soak in cold water with mild detergent. If needed, dab with diluted vinegar before washing.
Lipstick	Dab and blot the stain with rubbing alcohol, then launder as normal.
Meat	Soak in cold water with mild detergent, then clean normally.
Milk and Ice Cream	Soak in cold water with mild detergent, then clean normally.
Mustard	Soak in cold water with mild detergent, then clean normally.
Soda	Soak in cold water with vinegar or white wine before washing.
Tea	Rinse 15 minutes in cool water, then soak in enzyme pre-soak in warm water before washing.
Tomatoes or Catsup	Soak in cold water for 30 minutes, then rub liquid detergent directly into the stain and launder.
Wine	Sprinkle table salt on stain to absorb the wine, then sponge the stain with club soda, vinegar, or white wine. Blot and dry, then launder.